Schools have to produce an overview of progress in their pupils' learning, in the form of a summative assessment, at least once a year. National testing policies may or may not provide helpful support for this work, but they cannot supplant the responsibility of schools to provide regular summary guidance about the progress of each pupil's learning. Some see this task as an unfortunate necessity, and many experience a tension, between the formative practices which have been shown to enhance pupils' learning, and their own summative assessment requirements.

This booklet builds on work that the King's College London team have done in collaboration with teachers in three schools to develop ways of reviewing and improving their summative assessment methods. That collaboration developed a practical approach to this task; one which has shown that such development can forge consistent and positive policies which can establish mutually supportive relationships between formative and summative assessments. These relationships are part of an approach which treats assessment as an intrinsic part of effective teaching and learning.

In addition to reporting these positive findings, this booklet also shows how they are reinforced by a survey of reports of research and development projects from six other countries. These also show that wo [illegible] sta [illegible] use [illegible] developed, and produced similar positive effects on their teaching.

A finding common to those projects and to our own is that collaboration between teachers is essential to their professional development in assessment, and that work which such collaboration produces can both enrich the quality of their teaching and enhance teachers' confidence in their own assessment results.

Acknowledgements

Most of the guidance offered in this booklet derives from the collaboration of its authors with teachers in three schools in Oxfordshire. In this collaboration, we and the teachers explored how the principles of summative assessment and the ideas reported in the wide range of international literature about this topic, could be implemented within the everyday context of the schools. We can claim that the ideas that are set out here are practicable and rewarding because they emerged from the practical experience and the reflective insights of the teachers who worked with us. This work owes a great deal to these teachers, and to the support of their work by their schools and by the local authority. We also acknowledge the contribution of the Nuffield Foundation: their financial support was crucial in enabling us to carry out this work.

1. What does this booklet offer?

Previous booklets in this Black Box series have focused on teachers' formative assessment, indicating ways in which assessment can serve, at the heart of the day-to-day activities in the classroom, to improve pupils' learning. Such activities are central to every teacher's work, and many have welcomed ideas about ways to make their assessment more effective.

It would be surprising if all ideas about improving testing were to be welcomed with the same enthusiasm by everyone. While teachers have readily engaged with the guiding principles of formative assessment, we have found that they are less willing to look at changing their summative assessment practices. One major reason for this is the stress and pressures caused by externally imposed tests. School managements and parents require 'success' so that many teachers feel compelled to 'teach to the test' even though they admit that by so doing they are betraying their own values. A more fundamental effect of the political commitment to external accountability systems is that it suggests to teachers that many politicians, parents and even some of their own school's management, believe teachers' assessments of their own pupils are flawed and cannot be trusted. Is this scepticism justified?

In the UK, national inspectorates' reports have repeatedly identified assessment as the weakest aspect of the work of schools. Moreover, other countries have found that when externally imposed tests are abandoned, many teachers continue to use the same types of tests as the sole basis for their summative assessments. So, while teachers may have disliked the external tests, many were not confident that they could do better.

Does this matter? A concern frequently expressed by teachers who have been committed to improving assessment for learning is that at some point they have to change gear and teach to the test: the summative and the formative functions are seen at worst as irreconcilable, at best as uneasy bedfellows. A more supportive relationship would clearly be helpful for teachers and for their pupils.

But there are other reasons why teachers' lack of confidence in their ability to formulate effective tests matters. Teachers' assessment of their pupils is not just for external accountability, year-on-year results are important for the school management's assessment of individual teachers' work. Furthermore, advice to pupils and their parents about progress and about future choices among subjects, and communication to future teachers of the same pupils all depend on the summative assessments of current and past teachers. A notable example is the transition of pupils between any two stages, whether from primary to secondary, or between upper secondary stages.

More generally, policy-makers' distrust of teachers' abilities to assess should ideally be overcome in order for pupils and their parents to trust teachers in their turn. Such distrust can only be challenged if teachers and schools are confident that the skills, practices and policies underpinning the summative assessments they carry out can be trusted as fair to every pupil and comparable in standard within and between schools.

In principle, a school's own assessments should be more helpful to pupils than their marks on an external test. Indeed, since the teacher has numerous opportunities over a year's work with a class to observe each pupil's achievements and problems, it seems ridiculous that the evidence of a few hours' work in the artificial conditions of the formal written test be preferred to any evidence that the teacher can produce. Since teachers' are not subject to the same constraints of time and cost as external agencies, they ought to be able to take account of pupils' achievements in a range of contexts far broader than those of the formal written test. Thus, teachers' assessments should, in principle, be better able to meet the criteria of reliability, validity and comparability by which such agencies are themselves judged.

The purpose of this booklet is to set out ways in which the summative assessments created by teachers and their schools can be improved so that they comfortably meet the criteria upon which all such assessment should be judged. Its ideas and recommendations are based on two main sources. The first is our experience of, and findings from, a two-year development study with three secondary schools in England in which approximately 20 teachers of English and of mathematics worked in collaboration to improve the quality of their summative assessments and to establish that the results were fair and comparable across the three schools (Black et al. 2011).

The second source is the findings of published studies, notably from USA, Canada, Australia, New Zealand, Scotland and Wales. These studies show that the issues outlined above have been a cause for concern in many different state systems. Moreover, the different situations, and the innovations introduced in pursuit of reform described in these studies, help to broaden understanding of the problems involved and may assist in the development of ways to tackle them.

This booklet sets out its analysis and recommendations in the following sequence. *Section 2* gives a brief account of the roles of two main functions of assessment, *for* learning and *of* learning, within the whole enterprise of teaching and learning, and also outlines the five stages of any teaching activity. *Section 3* then considers the quality of assessments, exploring validity, reliability and comparability and the challenges that can undermine them.

These two brief sections serve to set up the background for *Section 4*, which describes a seven-step action plan for summative assessment, outlining the methods developed in our work with our group of teachers in England. It shows how teachers found that their active participation improved both the quality of their summative assessments and their confidence in the results that they produced. Our approach was not to seek to impose a new system but rather to look at the methods that teachers already used in their classrooms and then help them develop these in a more rigorous and dependable fashion. Our hope is that this booklet will help other teachers in a similar way. This help may be further enriched by the evidence and ideas in *Section 5*, which reflects on, and adds to, these findings in the light of further lessons that can be drawn from work from other countries, so leading to the summary of our main conclusions in *Section 6*.

2. Assessment inside the Black Box

Both formative and summative assessment are essential components of teaching and learning. In general terms, assessment is simply the production and interpretation of evidence of achievement. If this evidence is used to guide the next steps in progress, it is for learning, or formative; if it is used to sum up, judge, make decisions about, progress so far, it is of learning, or summative. The results of any assessment might serve both categories.

A unified view of the role of assessment in pedagogy can be presented in terms of the five stages involved in any teaching activity, as follows:

A. Formulating aims

This is the stage of strategic decision. All that follows should relate to a clear formulation of the learning aims.

B. Planning activities
The aims are to be achieved by choosing, adapting, or inventing activities which will engage pupils and thereby elicit responses from them which help to clarify and then extend their understanding.

C. Implementation
The way in which a plan is implemented in the classroom is crucial. What is needed is formative interaction which stimulates and builds on the pupils' contributions. Thus, implementation of a plan based on stated aims is the core activity of assessment for learning.

D. Review
At the end of any learning episode there should be a review, to check before moving on. The assessment used at this stage may be designed to be summative, but its results can also be for learning. An example is using peer marking to help all pupils to develop understanding of the criteria required to meet the aims. It may also help the teacher to identify a need to revisit some issues with the class as a whole.

E. Summing up
This is a more formal version of the Review stage above; here the results may be used to make decisions about a pupil's future work or career, to report progress to other teachers, school management teams and parents, and to report the overall achievements more widely to satisfy the need for accountability.

These five stages can interact in helpful ways. The experience of classroom implementation in stage C may lead to changes in the activities planned in stage B; the findings of a review in stage D could prompt a revision of the work in either, or both, of stages C and B. Stage E might go further, as the broader overview that should be characteristic of, say, an end-of-year assessment might indicate ways in which all four preceding stages should be reconsidered.

In addition to such *feed-back* of each stage to its predecessors, there should also be *feed-forward*. This second idea can make a very helpful contribution to teachers' planning of their work. For example, the design in stage B of a classroom activity will be informed by the teacher's experience of how a class is likely to respond to particular opportunities or challenges in stage C, while the problems arising in class discussion of a particular issue could guide the design of specific questions in a test to review that topic.

A more fundamental aspect of *feed-forward* is exemplified by the experience of most teachers that the only sure way to discern the precise intention of an externally prescribed curriculum or syllabus is to study 'past papers', for these are the best way to understand, and convey to their pupils, what they are meant to achieve. A school's own assessment and teaching plans could be used in the same way. The most effective way that teachers can clarify the learning aims of their teaching, and to communicate these to one another and to their pupils is to illustrate the meaning of those aims by the concrete examples of assessment items. Thus anticipation of assessment is a valuable part of stage A. This approach is further illustrated in the related practice, *front-ending*, referred to in *Section 6*.

The overall point of this five-stage approach is that teaching, learning, and assessment should all be closely interlinked in the planning and implementation of any teaching programme. To treat assessment as a marginal or secondary issue is to impoverish the work, by missing opportunities for improvement and cohesion.

3. Validity, Reliability and Comparability

The result of a summative assessment will be used by teachers, by each pupil, and by others involved with that pupil's future, to provide guidance, perhaps to make decisions. So what matters is that the use of the assessment evidence for these purposes is justified: this is the key concept of *validity*.

The following four features can undermine the validity of assessment results.

- The first is that the tasks or tests used may reflect only a fraction of all the aims and topics in the syllabus involved, that is, it uses only a small *sample* of all of the tasks which could have been set, and a pupil might have performed differently with a different sample.
- The second challenge to validity is that a pupil might have performed differently on the same tasks if they had been attempted on another day.
- The third problem is that a pupil might show a different performance with a different method of assessment, for example, in designing a science investigation with the real apparatus rather than in an exercise using only pictures of the apparatus, or in writing about a novel with the book on the desk rather than having to rely entirely on memory of the book.
- The fourth problem is that there may be ambiguities in the marking: these may be due to carelessness or to differences in the criteria used, or in their interpretation, by different markers.

All of these four can also be classified as threats to the *reliability* of an assessment. Enhancing reliability is an important requirement for enhancing validity, but it is not enough on its own. When all of the above have been separately tackled, the overall result may still be misleading because of a fifth limitation. A pupil may be very adept at tackling a range of the standard methods in a typical maths test, but be unable to deploy those methods in a problem which requires choice among several possible methods. In English, a pupil may be adept at writing about the set books for a course in the appreciation of literature, but be unable to develop an appreciation of a work that is not on the set menu. In science, a pupil might be able to describe standard laboratory experiments, but be unable to suggest an experimental method to check on a new hypothesis. In each of these cases, the inferences that can be made on the basis of the initial assessment might be seriously limited: the assessment is not valid as it does not require pupils' use of their learning in a range of contexts.

Finally, there is the need for *comparability* between the assessments of different teachers, both within any one school and between different schools. All who use assessment results need assurance that different teachers and their different schools are judging by the same criteria and by the same standards.

These discrete features all need attention if the overall aim, that users of assessment outcomes can confidently infer that those outcomes are valid, reliable and comparable, is to be achieved. It is also essential that the designers and the users of any assessment share the same understanding of the nature of the achievements signified by 'a good score' in that assessment.

The next two sections will explain in some detail the practical steps by which schools may tackle these five difficulties and meet the criteria of *reliability*, *validity* and *comparability*.

4. An Action Plan

There cannot be a single plan of action for the development of a school's summative assessment policy. Any such plan has to build upon existing practices and the particular strengths and weaknesses of each school. This section describes one example: the plan which our group developed during two years' work with three schools and around twenty teachers. However, as we will explain in the later section, so many of our findings were similar to those experienced in other countries and in other school subjects, that we are confident that we offer ideas which, with selection and adaptation, will be of value to any school and in any subject.

Our 'action plan' was composed as the work proceeded, and often modified as unexpected needs emerged. It owes a great deal to the teachers involved and some of its main features will be illustrated by quotations taken from reports written by those teachers. It is presented chronologically, so the main steps are discussed in the sequence in which the need to attend to them arose.

Step 1: The initial audit

Our first step was to review and audit each school's existing practices and policies. We explored the main end-of-year or end-of-term assessments, seeking answers to such questions as:

- How do different teachers produce evidence of the achievement of the pupils in their classes? What different types of evidence do they use for this purpose?
- What steps are taken to check the reliability and validity of this evidence? And what is done to ensure that, for example, the different teachers of any one year group, or the teachers who will teach those same classes in their subsequent year, are producing and using assessments which are comparable, both in the aims they assess and the criteria used?
- Who is responsible, within each subject and/or across each year group, and across the whole school, for oversight of these practices, and are all staff aware of these responsibilities?
- Do summative assessment practices have detrimental effects on the way teachers feel they should teach, or on the learning habits of their pupils? Do they favour any particular group of children? Do they cause undue stress for any individuals or groups?

We found that some schools could not give answers to these questions in ways that were satisfactory to themselves. Furthermore, in some cases, individual teachers were unaware of existing policy. On the other hand some schools and some subject departments had robust practices on which they could build.

However, it was found that, while teachers had well-established procedures, they had not reflected on whether the results genuinely justified the advice to, and decisions about, pupils which were then based on them, and they had little experience of the constraints and benefits that could follow from establishing comparability between their assessments. As one teacher put it:

...everybody in this department seems to do it in a very different fashion at the moment and it would be nicer to do it in a way that meant that we are all singing from the same hymn sheet if you like. I think it's made us think very carefully about how we construct our year and construct our year span in terms of what comes when and what's being assessed when.
(English teacher, Black et al., 2011, p461)

Step 2: Exploring validity

The findings of our initial audit led us to suggest that the next step should be to discuss the basic issue of the validity of assessments. This was done at the individual subject level, with subject teachers challenged to discuss their answers to the question: 'What does it mean to be good at X?', where X was English, or maths. When the groups had formulated their answers, the follow-up question was: 'Do the assessments we use at present reflect in practice our answer to the first question?'.

The project made me think more critically about what exactly I was assessing. The first

question I remember being asked ('what does it mean to be good at English?') gave me a different perspective on assessment. I find myself continually returning to this question.
(English teacher, Black et al., 2010, p222)

An exploration of validity is fundamental to the whole process of improvement. It can lead teachers to explore their own beliefs and values, or even to articulate them for the first time. Discussions on this theme helped each subject's teacher group to develop a shared understanding of why they thought it important pupils learn about their subject. A formulation of their agreed responses became the basis on which they developed their critique of the quality of their existing assessments, discussing whether these were fair and valid measures of the capabilities of their pupils. It formed the basis on which they sought to improve the quality of their practices, and evaluated the potential of any new assessment methods. One maths teacher reported on this process as follows:

The maths department of [School C] has in place a series of end of unit tests which, at the time, generated a series of numbers without any relation to areas of the national curriculum. The first thing that [colleague] and I did was to rewrite the tests in order that they generate useful information about how well students are doing in each area against national curriculum levels.
(Maths teacher, Black et al., 2010, p221)

What emerged here was that this work on the *Summing up* stage (stage E) had driven thinking back into considering the link between this stage and the initial stage A of *Formulating aims*.

This phase of the work led naturally to step 3 of our action plan. Given a realisation that present assessments should be improved, and with the target of achieving enhanced validity agreed, it was necessary to proceed in a systematic way to initiate and evaluate changes aimed at achieving this improvement.

Step 3: Evidence from tests and tasks

Clearly, any single piece of work could not adequately fulfil all the requirements of a thorough assessment, for it could not record achievement in all the learning aims in any one subject, so it could not meet the criteria for reliability and validity explained in the previous section.

Because of this, the teachers decided that each pupil would produce a portfolio: a collection of selected pieces of work that would give an overview of achievement over the year. The contents could include scripts produced in formal tests, pieces of coursework in written or other forms, and perhaps also video evidence or other artefacts where such items might be needed to secure validity.

In considering the evidence of achievement that should be included, it was soon clear that there was a wide range of possibilities, and that optimum choices would vary between one subject and another. Moreover, it was essential that the quantity of evidence collected for a portfolio be manageable. The discussion below reports on how the teachers of English and of maths arrived at their selections, starting with traditional formal tests and moving on to tasks undertaken in class.

Improving written tests

The first candidates to be considered for inclusion were written responses to test questions produced under formal test conditions. The teachers were familiar with such tests, and with the sources from which they could obtain test questions. While the English teachers were cautious, mainly because they thought that many test questions did not reflect their subject aims, the maths teachers were clear that these could play a useful role in the overall assessment of a pupil; as one maths teacher put it:

It all points towards the 'what does it mean to be good at maths?' question and how we [get] the students to show this – surely tests in a formal way (if properly constructed) have a role to play in allowing students to demonstrate this – and does also leave scope for teacher assessment – if the teachers are confident in this.

(Maths teacher, Black et al., 2010, p223)

It was also clear that, if they were to be included, these questions should be scrutinised carefully, in the first instance to explore their validity. In this scrutiny the English teachers paid particular attention to the criteria which they had developed in their initial exploration of validity. A teacher of English made this point in reflecting on the national tests which used to be set at age 14 in England:

I knew I hated the KS3 tests and found the preparation of students for these tests as one of the most unrewarding aspects of my job. However, through the project, I now have a much better understanding of why the tests are so problematic.

(English teacher, Black et al., 2010, p221)

As a related part of this scrutiny, teachers analysed the outcome when test questions had been tackled by a class in informal testing at the end of a topic. One obvious criterion to apply was whether some questions turned out to be too difficult or too easy: scrutiny of pupils' responses and comments by the pupils themselves helped pinpoint why some questions did not work well. Reasons often found were that the language used in some questions was not understood by all pupils, or that the question was misinterpreted so that some pupils produced good answers – but to a different question.

A less obvious feature was that some questions might not discriminate between those pupils whose understanding was clear and those whose understanding was uncertain. Such questions would lower the overall reliability of the test.

Appendix 2 describes a way of examining a set of the question scores for a group of pupils to identify which questions are discriminating and which may not be.

Classroom tasks – design and development

Tasks undertaken in class are another type of task that might be included within a portfolio of evidence.

Even after discussion of ways to improve the quality of formal or informal summative testing, it was still clear that some important aspects of validity could not be tested using such testing. Examples of problematic tasks were, in maths, selecting and trying out the contribution that different methods could make to an everyday problem or, in English, composing a piece of creative writing. The fact that such tasks would vary greatly across subjects was evident as issues arose in maths which were quite different from those that had to be tackled in English.

New tasks had to be tried out on a small scale. In this development work, the initial focus on engaging teachers in exploring validity provided important criteria:

It is important that teachers understand the skills that are being assessed (and make up what it is to be good at English) rather than being fixated on the form of the assessment. Teachers can then communicate the value of the assessment rather than just focussing on the test in isolation.

(English teacher, Black et al., 2010, p222)

What was found hard to predict was that a new task might turn out either to be too hard for, say, the lowest third of a class, or too easy for the highest group so that it might demoralise some pupils, or give no useful information about others. This problem could often be put right by modifying the task or its presentation.

Some other issues are illustrated by the following examples. One maths task required pupils to compare, describe and classify standard paper sizes (A0-A5)[1]. This task was successful in that it engaged and motivated the pupils:

I think one of the reasons is that it's a good task is that it's a real task. It's all based on A4, A5 and A6 you know, which is in real life, kids know that… they can physically hold up an A5 sheet against an A4… a lot of kids are engaged straight away… it's a piece of work that every kid could achieve from.

(Maths teacher, Black et al., 2011, p455)

While most pupils could explore and describe the relationships between adjacent paper sizes, they found it more demanding to show that these relationships required that the lengths of the two sides of each piece be in the ratio of $1:\sqrt{2}$. It was found that many students

---

[1] This task was invented by GAIM project – see Appendix 1.

had great difficulty writing up their work, perhaps because they had only limited experience of writing up mathematical activities of this kind.

In English, many teachers were already using realistic tasks which pupils could tackle in normal classroom conditions and which gave opportunity to develop creativity and flair in the use of language, and in the application of the skills they were learning. As any particular task was shared between teachers and tried out in practice, unexpected shortcomings often became evident. One of the key criteria that emerged was that a task should evoke evidence of the attainment it was designed to test:

...an essay tends to be all about their writing and weaker students just rely completely on a writing frame... the writing frame tends to be structured, structured to show their skills of inference where in fact you can't even see where they've got skills of basic retrieval in that essay. That's often done for them in the writing frame.

(English teacher, Black et al., 2011, p455)

Another difficulty related to student perceptions of work in English: students equate writing with work. However, struggles with such difficulties produced valuable results in that students became more aware of the objectives for a piece of writing and of how it would be assessed: they began, as one teacher put it, to gain 'insight into layers of meaning and recognising forms and being able to use them'.

Across both maths and English, we found that, as a result of teachers taking responsibility for their own tasks and involving their pupils more interactively in their production and their assessment, they developed new insights into their pupils' learning. Some such progress was linked to attempts to cover all the aims that validity required. The 'paper sizes' task in mathematics was an example. In English, the assessment of speaking and listening was difficult mainly because it had been neglected in the national tests in England for age 14.

Overall, the teachers we encouraged to work together did agree that the opportunities provided for collaboration on task construction had both improved their judgement of task quality and produced practically useful teaching materials. Appendix 1 gives a few further examples of tasks, in four subjects, and also reference to sources where others might be found.

Step 4: Designing pupil portfolios

It was important to ensure that all the teachers involved were using the same criteria and standards in making their assessment judgments. To achieve this, there had to be a procedure for comparing their assessments of the same samples of pupils' work. The samples used were portfolios: each pupil's portfolio was a collection of selected pieces of his or her work, and in order to make comparisons possible, the selection of the samples that were in such portfolios had to conform to agreed guidelines. It was clear that these portfolios could only serve their purpose if each contained a variety of examples of a pupil's work, and that decisions about the number of pieces of evidence required had to be agreed by all those involved in the assessment process. These components might be produced at different times during a school year, and local conditions might determine when they should be completed. The schools in the project generally opted for work produced as part of normal classroom work, a choice influenced by their wish to implement the new summative exercises alongside and in harmony with the formative practices they had already developed.

It was readily agreed that the portfolio should meet the criteria for reliability and validity as effectively as possible, while at the same time ensuring that pupils' time spent on the component tasks would make a positive contribution to their learning. For maths, one teacher expressed the aim as a need to 'cover all aspects of a varied and balanced diet'. So, for example, previous neglect of the area of statistics had to be corrected. Some teachers also wanted to explore the use of oral assessments to provide extra evidence about some pupils whose achievements in other components were inconsistent. The combination of open-ended classroom tasks with formal tests was regarded as essential to ensuring validity, but the test component was given more priority in maths than in English.

However, in English the issue of the neglect of some aspects in the past was a common cause for concern. An example was the need to produce separate assessment evidence about writing, reading, and speaking – as one teacher put it:

So, I feel like focus in the past has been largely on their writing. And I think the result of this project would be they would comment more on their reading skills and on their speaking and listening. I think it will mean a much richer and wider report.
(English teacher, Black et al., 2011, p457)

Despite the enthusiasm for its inclusion, the assessment of speaking and listening was seen as particularly problematic because it was difficult to collect and compare evidence about each individual in a group situation. There was also concern that group composition might enhance or inhibit an individual's opportunity to perform at their best level. To deal with this within the constraints of time and opportunity, teachers used their professional judgement to set up the optimum situation for each individual: if they suspected that a particular individual's performance had been hampered by the specific group they worked in, then they collected a second set of data on a second occasion. Such an approach also allowed teachers to create a back-up assessment for children who had been absent during the initial assessment activity.

A more general ambition was that tasks might be more varied than those used in the past, to match the varied interests and abilities of pupils, while being sufficiently similar to reflect achievements of the same aim.

It was foreseen that comparability of the outcomes, both within and between schools, would require some degree of consistency across all those portfolios which were to be compared. This requirement did not automatically lead to complete uniformity. Across the collaborating schools, the teachers in both subjects decided that some of the tasks should be the same for all, and that another specified number could be left to the choice of each teacher, with the only requirement being that a description of these tasks be freely available. An advantage of such transparency was that it could help in the development of new tasks which might eventually become suitable replacements for the original compulsory tasks.

It was finally agreed that in maths each portfolio would include, in addition to results from formal tests, the pupil's reports on six tasks, three to be the same across the schools to provide a basis for comparability, and the set to cover at least one in each of number and algebra, space and shape, and data handling, all to involve using and applying mathematics. The agreed specification in English also involved three common tasks, again requiring that all main sections of the curriculum, reading, writing (both fiction and non-fiction), and speaking and listening, be covered, using, for the latter two elements, group work, role play and public speaking.

The decisions about portfolio composition had to be agreed, within and then between schools, at an early stage in the school year because these decisions had to be implemented on many occasions during that year. Schools and teachers could focus on the optimum arrangements for themselves and their learners – they did not have to work to a framework imposed by an external agency.

Step 5: Comparability of tasks

The way in which pupils work at a task will depend on the way in which the task is presented to them. To ensure comparability of outcomes, two issues, *clarity* and *uniformity*, had to be considered.

Clarity became an issue when it was realised that pupils might take time to understand what was required of an unfamiliar task. So it was agreed that any portfolio task should not be completely novel – preliminary work on similar tasks should ensure that pupils were not disadvantaged through misunderstanding the requirements. One maths teacher commented on the outcome of such development of understanding as follows:

...at the end of units, they'd all be really nice investigations to do that would allow them to think about things that they've covered in class, but also, you know, be exposed to the investigations of how to do them, what to think

about. Because I was quite surprised at the beginning how they couldn't... they didn't know how to do it.

(Maths teacher, Black et al., 2011, p455)

A related argument concerned whether portfolio tasks should fit naturally into the teaching and learning work of a class. Any investment in 'preliminary work' could only be justified if the activities involved were a valuable part of the learning programme as a whole – indeed if this were not the case, the ensuing assessment could hardly be valid.

Such incorporation of portfolio tasks into the classroom had to be considered in the light of the need for the portfolio's evidence to be the pupil's own work. The following possibilities were considered – pupils might:

- collaborate in conducting a search, for relevant books in a library, for example, or for different types of plants in a field, and could work in groups to share and then discuss the resources they had assembled; they might then be required to write a piece about the project, individually and in controlled conditions;
- work together as a class on a particular project, such as the collection of resources for the design of a poster about a topic, and then be asked to work on their own in examination conditions to produce a poster on a different topic, being provided with a set of materials relating to that topic;
- work in groups on a problem and then present their conclusions orally to the class, sharing the presentation between them, with the teacher assessing on the basis of that evidence and recording the presentations on camera or voice recorder to support the portfolio record.

It was also suggested that while some tasks should involve pupils working in groups or pairs, others should involve individual endeavour; variety in performance across different degrees of collaboration could help the teacher to understand more fully the achievements of particular pupils in a range of different working contexts, thus providing a richer source of evidence for reporting to parents and senior leaders.

The more complete picture of present and potential achievement of pupils that was provided by a diverse range of tasks was crucial to securing the validity of any assessment. However, pupils had to be helped to realise that such tasks were as important as the more familiar formal tests.

These considerations about *clarity* overlapped with the need for *uniformity* in presentation: the achievements of pupils from different classes, and from different schools, could not be audited for comparability unless they had been presented in comparable ways. Without agreed guidelines, teachers noted that some might give more help than others, which could inflate the achievements of some children but was also likely to prevent some learners showing the full range of their understanding. However, our experience showed that even with honest attempts at fair presentation, problems could arise:

...I remember [colleague] and I doing the same task and obviously introducing it very differently and getting very different results. So I think having some agreed starting point is essential.

(Maths teacher, Black et al., 2011, p456)

Some felt that the best way of meeting this requirement would be to use identical presentations.

This question of uniformity of presentation was linked to consideration of the amount of help pupils might be given, both inside and outside the classroom, for here again, differences could undermine any fair comparison between pupils' work. There were two issues – help given to a whole class and help given to individual pupils. It seemed obvious that the latter should be ruled out in the case of a portfolio task: however, some argued that a teacher might notice, as a pupil worked on a task, that he or she had misunderstood the task's requirements so that what was produced would not be a fair example of what that pupil was actually able to do; in such a case, then, intervention could help ensure that the final assessment would be more fair so might be justified, even desirable. However, a record of any help should be attached to the pupil's work and allowed for in subsequent assessment.

Step 6: Authentic and comparable marking

The work described in step 5 above was the *first step* towards securing comparability by ensuring that the pupil portfolios were sufficiently uniform in their contents and their overall composition.

Given that teachers would select and mark or grade all of the work of their classes, the *second step* was to ensure that all those teaching the same subject and year group agreed to work to the same marking scheme for each piece of work. We found this more difficult than anticipated, mainly because such external guides as, for example, the levels statements in the national curriculum for English turned out to be imprecise on certain key aspects, so that there was a need for discussion, at an early stage and with examples of pupils' work, to achieve clarification. Similarly, in maths it was found that the published criteria applying to pupil investigations were too general; more detailed criteria were needed to distinguish reports which showed understanding from those which mentioned the appropriate terms and techniques but did not relate these to the task in valid ways.

Conversely, it was found that very tight schemes could make it hard to encourage and reward pupils' creativity. This feature varied between subjects. For example, in English, creativity and flair in a writing assignment could not be judged by an analytic approach: collaboration, drawing on agreed formulations about validity, helped teachers to rely more on their holistic judgments as one English teacher put it: 'Project has removed anxiety about delineating success only in terms of a neat, prescriptive check list'.

However, such judgements had to be defensible by reference only to the pupil's text. While a teacher who knew a pupil could read more into that pupil's work than any external assessor, agreement between different teachers could only be based on the actual text.

The *third step* towards achieving comparability was to give an overall mark or grade to a portfolio as a whole. Given that portfolios were composed so that the collections gave a broad and complete picture of each pupil's achievements, there was bound to be variability in the outcomes for some pupils, both between different classroom tasks, and between these and the results of formal tests. This indeed was a strength insofar as it meant that the portfolios were giving all pupils several different opportunities to show what they could achieve, but it made it hard to formulate agreed ways to arrive at an aggregate assessment of a collection of diverse pieces of evidence. Our experience was that different teachers tackled such problems in different ways. While some flexibility was needed, it was found necessary for any collaborating group to have agreed rules of aggregation: these included the different weights given to different components, and some rules about hurdles (so, for example, a failure in such a component means the overall cannot be greater than a C) and about compensation (for example, an outstanding effort on one of two components can lift the overall result from a B to an A). It was not possible to lay down general rules: the teachers in each group were the people best placed to make the appropriate rules.[2]

A collaborating group could not check all of the work assessed by their colleagues – so in a *fourth step*, groups formulated rules for selecting a few examples from the work of each teacher. These rules specified the numbers of examples to be produced, and the ways in which they should be distributed across the spectrum of grades: where the result was to produce a grade on, for example, a six-grade scale, it was helpful to choose borderline cases. It was not thought necessary to check every grade and every borderline; given that time, and concentration, would be limited, it was more rewarding to have a thorough appraisal of, say, two important

[2] The method explained in Appendix 2 for exploring the consistency across the different questions in a conventional test could also be applied to the set of (say) six items in a portfolio i.e. it might be useful to check whether some components place pupils in a very different rank order from others, and, where this occurs, to explore possible reasons.

borderlines than a more cursory look ranging over all of them.

The *fifth step* was the process of moderation, that is, a process in which a group of teachers discussed samples of one another's assessed work, gradually resolving their agreements and disagreements to arrive at an overall agreement. Most agreed that it would help the independence of the initial, i.e. separate, judgements of each teacher if the samples used contained no trace of any marking or grading already made by any teachers who had already arrived at their individual and independent judgements. Where this *blind marking* procedure was followed, the moderation meetings started with a report from every member of their independent judgements; this helped to identify those aspects in most need of discussion. One of the most frequent causes of discrepancies was the inadequacy of the available criteria: the gaps created by their vagueness had to be filled by personal judgement, so differences were bound to follow.

In these moderation meetings, teachers were often surprised to discover the wide differences between the judgements of colleagues about the same samples of work, even when the criteria had seemed clear. The outcome was that, in a few cases, teachers had to go back and scale up or down some of their original results.

One difficulty here was expressed as follows by one teacher:

I think that raises issues, you know, personal issues about people feeling that their judgement is being questioned or being undermined, or feeling that there are people in that public setting who are questioning what they are doing.

(Maths teacher, Black et al., 2011, p459)

This question over teachers feeling their judgement was being questioned arose in one department where comparability exercises of this type had not previously been deemed necessary. A pre-determined procedure, backed by a school policy, would have helped in coping with such problems. It was clear that working together making judgements on specific pieces of work helped teachers to interpret assessment criteria across a range of contexts, and through professional dialogue reach new understandings of assessment protocols and procedures.

Confidence in the final results, on the part of teachers, pupils, parents, and schools overall, was enhanced through the cooperation of the three schools in inter-school moderation meetings. This confidence developed because of the agreed procedures about uniformity of the portfolios, about the criteria on which assessments were to be based, about the rules for sampling and about the blind-marking procedure. Such sharing could lead to a positive evolution of each school's assessment practices:

...and we've had moderation meetings, we were together with the other schools, teachers

in other schools looked at how rigorous our assessment would be and they criticised what, you know, our marking criteria (are). And we changed it, which is all been very positive.

(Maths teacher, Black et al., 2011, p459)

Some of the teachers of English had prior experience of a particular moderation procedure, called *standardisation*, which involved initial training shared by all schools on a common set of examples, after which schools were assumed to be competent in applying common criteria and standards to their own work. Since the English teachers were familiar with this standardisation procedure, they argued that, once common exemplary materials had been collected and used as a basis for agreement, less rigorous procedures might be used, for example, in less frequent inter-school exercises. We found that maths teachers, who had not experienced this approach, were content, for their first work on comparability, to operate within the full moderation procedure, which was more rigorous in requiring both intra- and inter-school meetings every year, using the 'blind marking' procedure.

Step 7: Evaluation of the outcomes

The aim of this project was to develop and evaluate ways to help teachers improve the quality of summative assessments by making changes in their practices and strategies at individual, departmental and school level. To help us to evaluate the outcomes, we asked teachers to write their personal accounts of what they had learned from the work. We report here, with little or no comment, some extracts from these personal accounts which we have selected to give a fair overall picture of their view of the effects of the work.

The impact on pupils

I think it changed the dynamics of the lesson a little bit, in terms of well, in terms of there being much more an element of them getting on trying to find out… they were trying to be more independent, I think, I think some of them struggled with that, and others… some of them, some still find it quite difficult if they are not hand held all the way through. When others were happier to sort of, go their own way.

(Maths teacher, Black et al., 2011, p460)

…the kids felt it was the best piece of work they'd done. And a lot of teachers said 'ok we're really pleased with how they've come out', it's seemed to really give kids the opportunity to do the best that they could have done… Er, it just, the lower end kids it organises their work for them, it's basically a structured path for them to follow.

(English teacher, Black et al., 2011, p460)

The impact on parents

But, I think if all the teachers had more, possibly more ownership of what we are actually doing in terms of summative assessment, then you would have more confidence in saying to parents, which I think is one of the biggest things I find with lower school.

(Maths teacher, Black et al., 2011, p460)

'It provides you with convincing, comparative material and it's something that I have taken to meetings, with parents of students in classes other than my own. Being able to say, 'well this is what John's been able to do and this is why he is still on a 5C and not a 6A' and parents seem to react well to that...'
(English teacher, Black et al., 2011, p461)

The impact on teachers

The work alerted teachers to the need to be more aware of the weakness in their previous procedures, but because this meant new ways of working were needed, there were initial doubts:

Implementation of tasks – staff were a bit reluctant to do the projects... but post projects their views changed and this year development of investigation based tasks has become an issue that the KS3[3] staff have been keen to do and is being done as part of performance management.
(Maths teacher, Black et al., 2011, p461)

Several other benefits of collaboration were identified, for example:

...that the moderation and standardisation process was incredibly valuable in ensuring rigour, consistency and confidence with our approach to assessment; that teachers in school were highly motivated by being involved in the process that would impact on the achievement of students in their classes (like the moderation and standardisation at GCSE).
(English teacher, Black et al., 2011, p459)

One school planned to have such meetings three times a year. Some were considering the possible value of meetings to 'moderate formatively', that is, to develop shared judgements and criteria in advance of the occasions where decisions would have to be taken.

There were two more fundamental effects. One was that, because the broader focus of their assessment work gave pupils opportunities to achieve in diverse ways, the results also suggested new ways in which their teachers could improve engagement and motivation.

...you could see quite a lot from what people do, from how much work they put in outside of the classroom... and you can see quite a lot about how they think, as well, and how they work in groups is quite interesting.
(Maths teacher, Black et al., 2011, p459)

The second major effect was that the time devoted to improving assessments was more rewarding than expected because it enriched the whole range of the teachers' professional development. As one teacher explained:

I think it's quite a healthy thing for a department to be doing because I think it will

[3]KS3: Key Stage 3, a classification used in some UK schools to describe the first three secondary school years from ages 11–14.

encourage people to have conversations and it's about teaching and learning... it really provides a discussion hopefully as well to talk about quality and you know what you think of was a success in English. Still really fundamental conversations.
(English teacher, Black et al., 2011, p461)

In summary, our overall experience was that the project improved the confidence of all concerned in the standards reflected in each school's assessments. Moreover, efforts invested in the procedures it developed had brought a wide range of rewards. The work had helped the teachers to re-think their own understandings of criteria and standards, and to improve the rigour and consistency of their judgements, in ways that would ultimately have a positive impact on the achievements of their students.

5. Just one project: is there other evidence?

While the account in the previous section concerned ideas that emerged during one project, our approach to that project was influenced by similar work in other countries. In some studies, summative practices newly developed by schools and teachers were evaluated by systematic research, which has enriched our findings and also makes it possible to generalise from them with more confidence.

The purpose of this section is to describe some of the lessons which emerge from work in Australia, Canada, New Zealand, Scotland, the USA and Wales. The various state contexts range from those where authorities are implementing new ways to strengthen the role of teachers' summative assessments, to those with systems which have developed over more than 30 years. For assessments before the school-leaving age, some leave these entirely to teachers, some complement them with light-sample surveys, some require the use, in part or in whole, of national tests – perhaps drawn from national question banks. Assessment for 'high-stakes' school-leaving certificates, ranges from zero use of school-based assessments to almost complete reliance on them (in Queensland), with various combinations between these extremes. For us, what is relevant is how the findings of these studies provide helpful advice for schools wishing to improve their own assessments; to this end, these findings will be summarised in the following sub-sections.

Assessment systems in the UK and elsewhere

Most of information useful to us derives either from state initiatives developed over several years, or from more local initiatives in which agencies outside schools have helped small groups of schools by initiating, supporting and evaluating new ventures; into which category, incidentally, our own project falls. Some national initiatives have faltered because of the lack of an overall plan to link to a single coherent policy all those agencies which constrain schools. The use of the teacher-assessed component of the main school-leaving examinations in England has seen a cycle of new approaches followed by perceived failures and yet another new approach. However, the planning for these has, 'consisted of little more than pamphlets which were long on generalisation and short on practical suggestions.' (Daugherty, 2010, p389).

The same author has argued that in Wales, the lack of an infrastructure of support for teachers has hampered a policy which looked to replace the national tests by teachers' own summative assessments.

For Scotland, the history has been more complicated. A successful programme to help teachers develop assessment for learning (Hallam et al., 2003) was followed by a plan to leave all summative assessment, up until the school-leaving years, in the hands of schools. A requirement of schools to report achievement on the basis of tests composed of items drawn from a national assessment bank was cancelled: schools were free to use their own systems. At the same time, a light-sampling survey was developed to provide an overall national picture of achievement. However, there was no national programme to develop teachers' skills in summative assessment. The national inspectorate continued to emphasise the importance of using external test instruments, and local authorities were responding to national requirements to report progress by asking schools for their summative evidence. Most schools, lacking support for and confidence in their own assessments, continued their previous practice of reporting only on the basis of the externally provided tests. The exceptions arose where local groups of schools started to engage in inter-group moderation of their assessments, to help build both expertise and confidence (Boyd and Hayward, 2008). Another need has been highlighted by a national study of the transition of pupils between the primary and secondary phases of schooling. This has shown that the information about pupils' progress which was being provided by primary schools was inadequate in many cases, and was often ignored. This particular failing threw light on a more general weakness in the use of summative assessment to help the transition of pupils between successive years within schools. A detailed report on the situation has concluded with a set of recommendations for development of a national system (Hayward et al., 2012).

Such tensions have been found elsewhere. While the long established systems in several states in Australia, notably Queensland, were until recently, free of such tensions, recent changes in New Zealand (Crooks, 2011) with new requirements for schools to report to government on pupils' progress against national standards have created tensions, even when the means of assessment have been left wholly or largely in the hands of schools. One reason for this is suggested by three studies of schools' summative assessments, which showed that most of the schools studied did not collect, share or analyse evidence of their pupils' achievements in any systematic way; thus, choices or analyses of learning materials, or evaluation of any changes, were not informed by evidence of pupils' progress, and where teachers had developed skills of interpreting data, they did not relate outcomes to student progress. By contrast, systematic procedures were found to be rewarding:

Similarly, teachers who examined student data together and worked out as a group what its implications were for deciding how best to help those under-achieving, difficult-to-move students, had higher achieving students than those schools where such a collective examination, diagnosis and problem-solving cycle did not operate.

(Parr and Timperley, 2008, p69)

Overall, these various studies underline two main points. The first is that the findings of the initial audit in our work should not have been surprising, and that for schools who do audit, they will need models of effective systems against which the results can be evaluated and used to support further improvement. The second is that where time and effort have been devoted to helping teachers develop their assessments, their confidence and skills have improved quite markedly, and the improvements in their summative assessments have been of benefit, to their teaching as a whole and to their students.

We shall now examine specific aspects of the collected evidence gathered from overseas studies.

The quality of tasks

A key feature reported in many studies of assessment is the challenge of assembling a set of tasks, each of which assesses the range of curriculum aims, engages the pupils, and discriminates over a range of achievements. A common difficulty here is that while teachers are familiar with content-oriented tests, they lack experience and training in the assessments of deeper understanding and the ability to apply skills which validity demands.

In a project to develop assessment practices with a group of maths teachers in the USA, Webb (2009) found that their practice had been to use items for which the answer would simply be either correct or incorrect. Such items revealed little about their pupils' learning: when teachers started to use more complex and realistic items, they found it difficult to interpret their pupils' answers, but that more was learnt from them about the pupils, particularly from the justifications they gave for these answers. Interpretation skills were improved by requiring the teachers to solve mathematics problems that were, for them, demanding, and then to discuss with one another the formal or informal methods they themselves used in tackling these problems.

Another, and related, finding of his work was reported by Webb as follows:

However, while these materials are necessary to support change in classroom assessment, teachers are unlikely to learn how to use such materials effectively without reflecting on their current assessment practices and re-grounding such practices in principles that help articulate what it means to understand mathematics and how student understanding can be assessed.

(p2–3)

This illustrates the central importance of validity as a guiding criterion for improvement.

Some state authorities have tried to tackle the need for high-quality questions by setting up banks of well-tried items or tasks. In some cases, a general collection has been supplemented with a few items selected as special 'exemplars' to illustrate the meaning of key aims of the curriculum. Mark schemes have also been used, sometimes with sample pupil responses to show how such schemes are applied. However, most teachers find it necessary to amend such questions to fit in with their own teaching plans and to match the needs of their classes. Such adaptation is more manageable where teachers share their own questions with one another; a further step has been to encourage teachers to use a mixture of items they have composed with items from a central bank, and here again, having colleagues comment on their items, and perhaps try them out in several classes, which helps to evaluate and improve the quality. While the relevance of some of these outcomes will depend on the state systems within which schools operate, all reports stress the value of building collaboration through which teachers help one another in appraising, amending and evaluating possible tasks. Appendix 1 gives information about websites which provide banks of assessment items.

The teachers' task of selecting and assembling items for assessing their own classes calls for further professional development. In such selections, teachers must consider the match between their curriculum aims and tasks in which achievement of those aims can be expressed in concrete form. It is sometimes reported that sets of assessment exercises assembled by teachers to match curriculum aims are found, on external scrutiny, to have neglected some aspects of the curriculum and over-emphasised others. This additional responsibility for assessment and the requisite consideration of relating assessment to curriculum aims then affects pedagogy, as teachers will want to teach in ways that support this relationship.

Composing portfolios

For summative assessment purposes, a collection of tasks in a portfolio is usually found necessary. These would be the main evidence upon which assessment is based and, as emphasised in the earlier section, can only be the basis for dependable assessment if each contains a carefully selected set of work which represents the achievements of each pupil. Some states in the USA have aimed to assess schools by use of pupil portfolios. At the outset, it was often found that there were such wide differences between the collections from different schools that comparability was impossible; in other cases, a combination of clear specifications of contents and professional development training to help teachers to develop and apply scoring criteria has led to a satisfactory system.

The range of purposes which portfolios might serve is illustrated in the review of content-selection frameworks by Simon and Forgette-Giroux (2010). In one reported example, a portfolio for the assessment of writing had to include, for grade 12 (age 17) pupils, a reflective letter; a narrative or descriptive piece; an explanatory, exploratory, or persuasive essay; a research paper; and an interpretive or evaluative piece. Accounts from other subjects showed that each requires its own type of framework. What seemed common across the examples was that it is both vital and difficult to achieve the main aim, which should be to provide as complete a record as possible of each pupil's achievements.

Of particular interest is that some policies have required the involvement of the pupil in the collection and presentation: while such a collection may be constrained in requiring the choice to meet certain criteria, it can be enriched by requiring each pupil both to justify his or her selection and to include a reflective response, such as a self-assessment of the work.

Marking and moderation

Many teachers take on the extra work of marking for national large-scale assessments. One detailed study, of teachers marking responses to national literacy tests in Canada (Gambell and Hunter, 2004), found that teachers who had hitherto seen tests and marking as an exclusively summative exercise began to realise that these also carried lessons about classroom formative work. This realisation was strengthened by the experience of working with other teachers, and by seeing the responses from a wide range of pupils and schools, experiences which helped them to analyse responses more carefully in order to help their own pupils. Others realised that they could share the criteria and their experience of marking with their pupils. Overall, teachers' self-confidence in their own assessment work was enhanced – they were no longer 'lone professionals'. Similar benefits have been noted to have derived from moderation meetings in our project. However, the experience of marking large-scale formal testing cannot on its own help teachers develop the professional skills and language needed in assessing the range of pupils' achievements which such tests cannot assess.

Whether intra-school or in state systems, marking standards can only be fair to all pupils if different teachers are working to the same standards. The differences in judgement that arise when teachers engage in group moderation help concentrate attention, as one teacher found:

Ah, probably I would have needed to – and I will next time – is read that level B and C closer, you know, because the word were 'or' and 'and' in the end, and it took a few scripts to realise what the difference is.

(Connolly et al., 2011, p16)

However, there are more difficult problems involved, as the following reflections by teachers involved in a moderation discussion illustrates (quoted by Wyatt-Smith et al., 2010):

M2: I think you'll find we are agreed 90% on students A, B, C, D and E, except if you refer to that thing [the guide].
M1: So this is the last one.
M2: No, no, except if you refer to that document. We are agreed on the student's ability.
M1: And that's what they all say, a lot of people have criteria and standards they carry around in their head.

(p70)

The same authors report the following from a post-moderation interview of a teacher:

When we were stuck whether to give them like a D or an E, or a C or a D, um, someone in the group was always able to pluck out, um. The pertinent point that could get us across the line one way or another and everyone else would just, would just go 'yep, that's right, that's it' and so that was really good and I don't think you can come to that by yourself.

(p66)

Even with carefully designed criteria and scrupulous attention to these, no limited and explicit statement can replace the judgement of equivalence which the range and variety of pupil responses will always demand. In a study of their task of marking the course work component of GCSE assessment, Crisp (2011) found that experienced teachers and moderators used a combination of two approaches: one analytic – matching details to criteria; the other 'configurational' – looking more holistically at overall aspects of quality; for the latter they were drawing on past experience of examining many types of work. Teachers new to the work tended to work in the analytic mode only.

Sadler expressed the problem very clearly:

Use of natural-language descriptions together with exemplars is unlikely to provide a complete substitute for, or render superfluous, the tacit knowledge of human appraisers, simply because external formulations cannot be exhaustive and cover every conceivable case [nor would we want them to].

(Sadler, 1987, p201)

This does not mean that such tacit knowledge cannot be shared and honed by discussion between experienced professionals. A community of teachers can come to a common judgement even if their shared understanding cannot be set down in an explicit formula which would communicate to those without their professional experience.

This view, that moderation is a means by which teachers learn, is spelt out in more detail by a study of the experience of primary school teachers in New Zealand. The starting point was the introduction of a national requirement that teachers report to parents on the progress of their pupils in relation to new national standards. As the authors (Hipkins and Robertson, 2011) explained:

…the introduction of standards requires primary teachers and schools to investigate the meaning of the work that students generate. While teachers have always made judgements informally, moderation as an organised process requires making collaborative decisions to reach consensus agreements, and hence has become an important professional responsibility for all New Zealand's primary school teachers.

(p5)

The resources on which moderation meetings could draw were not only the standards, state guidelines, and examples of pupils work (described below as 'referents'), but also an 'accumulating and collective awareness' of these resources and of the teachers' new task.

Teachers bring their own working knowledge to the manner in which they draw on these referents during moderation and it is through the experience of sharing and negotiation that shared meanings and understandings can be created.

(p18-19)

Such shared understandings were only built slowly. One problem was that teachers had to resolve concerns about distinguishing between effort and achievement, about using – or not – personal knowledge of pupils (including particular challenges some pupils may have faced) of which there was no apparent evidence in the work being assessed, and about their conflicting beliefs about what the 'average' pupil should be able to achieve. These authors also drew attention to another difficulty:

Sharing and challenging one's own and others' beliefs can make people feel vulnerable and anxious so it is important that practice opportunities are conducted in a trusting and supporting environment.

(p20)

The overall conclusion of Hipkins and Robertson was that there was evidence that the moderation work had the potential for powerful professional learning, although it was too soon to be able to evaluate the consequent effects on pupils' learning.

Involving pupils

It is very easy to present pupils with assessment tasks in which their brevity or poverty of response shows that they cannot relate at all to the task. One of the most difficult challenges of assessment, whether *of* or *for* learning, is to ensure that the tasks explore the range of knowledge and understanding of pupils who may appear to be unable to demonstrate any capability. This difficulty was expressed in the following account of work with teachers in Australia, aimed at helping them to involve all pupils in their learning work:

...probably the biggest learning for a lot of our teachers was the scope of the task that they were asking the kids to do and just understanding the burrowing down, drilling down of that was what the biggest learning I think for a lot of our teachers, what they were asking for their kids to do, from the beginning, was just miles too big, we were trying to achieve too much and for some of our teachers that was the biggest learning they had, the awareness of what the kids knew before.

(Wyatt-Smith and Bridges 2008, p45)

It is obvious that teachers should try to share with pupils their understanding of the learning aims of the curriculum; for pupils, as for teachers themselves, such understanding cannot be achieved by explaining at an abstract level, but rather by building up understanding through discussion of assessment exercises and their associated marking. Failure to achieve such understanding of the learning aims can create a barrier for some pupils – a point that was expressed in rather stark terms as follows:

Some students succeed in negotiating these, apparently drawing on resources other than those that the teachers provide. Others may spend the compulsory years [of schooling] in an environment that is essentially conducted in a foreign language in which they never gain sufficient proficiency. And students need to be fluent to negotiate the ever more demanding literacy-bound assessment requirements successfully... assumption of students' curriculum literacies is not sufficient. These need to be incorporated in direct instruction.

(Wyatt-Smith and Cumming 2003, p58)

Concentration on this task, of using assessment examples to explain the purpose of the curriculum, was found to be rewarding:

...I think to a certain extent that we've empowered students in the learning process because there's not secret teacher's business anymore in terms of what the expectations are, that students are becoming very au fait with the criterion and being able to apply them in their own work.

(Wyatt-Smith and Bridges 2008, p61)

A similar positive effect was reported in a study of teachers' assessment practices in 36 New Zealand schools (Harris and Brown, 2009), as one primary teacher explained:

...once they understand that (shared assessment criteria) and they start applying it, then they've got that, 'Oh, I can see where I have to go next. I don't have to have the teachers tell me'. And that's what we've just started doing now is like, 'You tell me what you want me to do with the lesson? What are your weak areas that you don't understand?' so they've just started doing that.

(p376)

It might be argued that this is simply 'teaching to the test'. However, there is nothing wrong with such orientation of teaching, provided the test is a valid assessment of those learning aims which teachers value; the negative effects only arise when the tests are of very restricted validity.

A different, but related perspective, was presented by a study of the work of US high-school students aged 15 to 17, in English and in anatomy (Brookhart, 2001). These students were more successful and articulate than average, so it was not a representative sample; they were interviewed about their experience of 'assessment events', this term covering both the formative and the summative episodes they had experienced. The summative work included written tests in both subjects, practical exercises in anatomy and, in English, writing about a topic which they had researched and other forms of creative writing. The main finding was that pupils did not make clear distinctions between the formative and summative events, but regarded both as helpful; the former for developing general learning skills, the latter as useful preparation for future study. Overall, the perspective was that their learning was helped by cyclical interaction between the two and not obstructed by tension between them.

6. The main outcomes of our study

If we had to select two overall features of our own work which emerged as both surprising and very significant, they would be the stimulus given by the work to new thinking by teachers about the linking of *assessment with curriculum and pedagogy*, and the benefits for teachers of *learning through collaboration*. Both these features have also emerged strongly in international initiatives which have set out to develop teachers' summative assessments and they may be summarised as follows.

Assessment, curriculum and pedagogy

All aspects of expertise in assessment are obviously involved in the practice of summative assessment: the discussion in earlier sections focused on linking the general concept of validity to the audit of particular assessment methods, and about developing shared interpretations of standards criteria. However, more is involved than simply assessment techniques.

For example, in the practice of 'front-ending', assessment activities that will serve to provide evidence that students are achieving the planned aims are formulated at the same time as the aims themselves are being formulated. Such work to link planning, aims and evidence explores and develops the essential links between curriculum and summative assessment, and since it should also affect the teaching more directly through assessment for learning, it should also connect with pedagogy in a wider sense. This broader linkage was developed in two different studies. In the USA study mentioned above, it was found that:

Unfortunately, teachers often develop a set of classroom routines with little opportunity to examine and reflect on their concepts of classroom assessment and how this informs their decisions about the selection and design of questions and tasks, how they interpret student responses, and how to respond to students through instruction and feedback.

(Webb, 2009, p11)

Webb developed this point further in work with another group:

Furthermore, as teachers adapted practices, they began to re-think the learning objectives of their curricula and the questions they used during instructional activities.

(p14)

In reporting their work with teachers in a study with teachers in Queensland, Wyatt-Smith and Bridges (2008) described a similar finding:

So basically once you have the assessment firmly in place the pedagogy becomes really clear because your pedagogy has to support that – that sort of quality assessment task… that was a bit of a shift from what's usually done, usually assessment is that thing that you attach on the end of the unit whereas as opposed to sort of being the driver which it has now become.

(p48)

Such analyses suggest the value of thinking in terms of a cycle of assessment design, which starts with assembling items, then proceeds by analysing the responses produced when pupils attempt them; this may lead to the need to adapt either the items themselves, the teaching approach, or both, even down to rethinking the meaning of the aims, so leading back to a repetition of the cycle. This idea is related to the scheme of stages A to E outlined in *Section 2*, above.

Collaboration

The second major finding of our work concerns the positive effects of inter-school collaboration. These have already been highlighted in the account of our own project and have also been found in work that has adopted a similar approach. To quote just two comments from one such study:

It was a really good process. I think the conversation bit of the process was the most valuable part.

(Connolly et al., 2011, p14)

This study worked in part with schools in isolated, rural districts, where travel to meetings was very restricted; teachers and researchers explored the use of ICT to promote video conferencing – with very positive results:

...so I think, yeah, it's certainly very valuable for – especially for those schools where they're not, or they can't get that moderation process at the school level, but even when you do, I think it's really good, because we don't just talk to other schools in other regions, it just doesn't happen, so I think it's really good to have that.

(Connolly et al., 2011, p19)

Intra-school and inter-school collaboration has been emphasised throughout this document; such collaboration has been taken for granted, or explored and found rewarding, in innovative work in many countries. It is particularly important in an area such as summative assessment, where teachers' understanding, skills and confidence have been undermined by a combination of unhelpful national policies and neglect of the topic in the initial and in-service training of teachers.

The teacher's role

Any reform in education can only succeed if teachers play a central role in its development, and they can only exercise this role powerfully if they share their experience and resources. The study of the development of assessment underlines this point:

Any change to assessment processes (or in fact any educational reform) hinges on support from teachers, and support for teachers, to ensure an ability to adapt at classroom level... This requires theoretically-based yet practically-situated learning rather that decontextualised one-shot professional development.

(Wyatt-Smith and Masters 2007, quoted by Gunn 2007, p59)

The same argument has been central to this booklet, and we sum up our message by repeating the points made in our opening section:

- teachers and schools have the prime responsibility of assessing their pupils at frequent intervals throughout their school career;
- their assessment practices must serve the learning and the guidance of pupils in a valid, reliable and comparable way;
- the professional development needed to achieve the above can only be provoked and or guided in a general way by agencies outside the schools; help from external 'experts' can clarify understanding of the issues involved and stimulate innovation, but...
- the tough work of forging a fruitful coherence between assessment,

curriculum and pedagogy within any school's overall learning policy has to be worked out between teachers themselves, and between collaborating schools, in ways that are productive within their own contexts.

Appendix 1: Sample tasks from English, science, mathematics, and modern foreign languages

English tasks

1 Explore how Shakespeare uses staging devices in order to create tension in Act 3 scene 1 of *Romeo and Juliet*.

2 *Oral response in a group discussion.* From the book, *Holes*, discuss whether or not Camp Green Lake was a positive experience for Stanley.

3 *Fiction writing.* 'Falling': based on your reading of the story of Icarus, produce a witness' description of the event.

4 *Literary criticism essay.* Compare how two poets develop protest in their poems, examining the use of poetic techniques.

Science tasks

All are practical investigations.

1 **Bouncing surfaces:** Balls bounce better on some surfaces than on others. Some people claim that any ball which bounces best on one surface will also bounce best on other surfaces. Choose three different surfaces and three different types of ball and make tests to check whether or not this claim could be true.

2 **Insulation** against loss of heat is achieved by use of insulating materials. Obtain pieces of three materials, for example, from an old blanket, from discarded clothes, or from bubble wrap, which may be used to keep people, or hot drinks, warm. Devise a way to compare how effective your three materials might be in keeping a hot drink warm as long as possible.

Would your results apply to the task of selecting a material for making warm clothing for people?

3 **Dissolving:** Salt will dissolve in water and in vinegar. Devise and use a method to find out whether more salt will dissolve in vinegar than in water. Then apply it to test the dissolving of salt in other liquids.

Further ideas can be seen in http://www.nationalstemcentre.org.uk/elibrary, look for King's, then Beyond Fair Testing.

Mathematics tasks

1 How many different (cross-, T- and L-shaped) spaces are there on square and rectangular shaped grids of tiles? Represent your results by algebraic formulae relating your results to the numbers of tiles in each of the dimensions of a rectangular grid.
2 Compare, describe and classify standard paper sizes (A0-A5) in terms of the ratios of their side lengths and their areas, and consider the advantages of these relationships.
3 Compare different newspapers (such as tabloid, broadsheet, local) by generating and investigating a hypothesis using simple descriptive statistics.

Further ideas can be seen in http://www.nationalstemcentre.org.uk/elibrary search for GAIM resources, then GAIM activities: practical problems.

Modern Foreign Languages tasks

1 *Year 7 French*: Groups are asked to create a Sooty and Sweep and Co. puppet show that brings together all the language items they have been practising for the topic 'About me' – plus a bit more! – and use this to peer-teach visiting Year 6 pupils when they come for their French lesson.
2 *Year 11 German*: Create a topic revision 'brick in the wall' for a class revision 'topic wall' to include language content, sample answers for written tasks and role-plays, and suggested learning strategies.
3 *Year 9 Spanish*: Imagine you are on holiday in Spain and have to see the doctor. When you are in the clinic, you are asked to translate for someone who knows no Spanish and can only act out how they feel ill.

Appendix 2: Analysing a set of marks

The table below shows a set of marks from an eight-question test. The pupils A to F have been set out in order of the total marks – so Mary had the highest with a total of 54, and Craig the lowest with a total of 36. The mean mark for each question is shown at the foot of each column. The analysis involves taking a closer look at the marks for each question. The method is to add, for each question, the marks of the top third of the pupils, and then add separately the marks of the bottom third of the pupils: so for question number one, the scores of Mary and Ali (A+B) total 12 marks, those of pupils Saheera and Craig (E+F) total 11 marks. The same calculation has then been done for question two, and so on.

The point of doing this is shown by comparing the result for questions one and two: there is almost no difference between the two totals for number one, but there is a big difference for question two.

So the next step is to look separately at the top third and bottom third marks for each question. It is clear that numbers three, five and eight show, like number two, a big difference between the top and bottom third – these four discriminate. Numbers four, six, and seven are like number one, showing very little difference. The last two columns on the right show what happens if you split the total mark for each pupil into the total for the two, three, five and eight, and the total for one, four, six and seven. It is then clear that the rank order is determined by the former group, and that the latter are a weak group in that they do not contribute at all to this rank order.

This diagnosis shows that some questions may be working as intended, others are not. One can then look at the weak questions to see why they don't work as intended. Number seven may just be too easy, and number four too hard, but numbers one and six are more puzzling. The point overall is that this simple analysis can lead those who set the questions to look more closely at them, and perhaps also at the pupils' responses, to learn why some seem to work well and others do not, and the findings may help to improve a test in the future.

The other point is that, while eight questions might, between them, have sampled most of the topics in the subject being tested, the test is in fact

		QUESTIONS								SUM Of all	SUM 2,3,5,8	SUM 1,4,6,7
		1	2	3	4	5	6	7	8			
Mary	A	*7*	7	9	*4*	8	4	9	6	**54**	30	24
Ali	B	*5*	9	4	*3*	9	6	6	4	**46**	26	20
Louis	C	*8*	3	4	*6*	6	2	7	7	**43**	20	23
Allen	D	*4*	4	3	*2*	7	8	9	5	**42**	19	23
Saheera	E	*4*	5	5	*7*	3	3	9	3	**39**	16	23
Craig	F	*7*	3	4	*1*	5	7	7	2	**36**	14	22
Means		**5.8**	**5.2**	**4.8**	**3.8**	**6.3**	**5.0**	**7.8**	**4.5**	43.3	**20.8**	**22.5**
Sum A+B		*12*	16	13	*7*	17	10	15	10		56	44
Sum E+F		*11*	8	9	*8*	8	10	16	5		30	45

only assessing four of them. If the four faulty questions could be amended or replaced by better ones, the effective sample would be eight. So this analysis is relevant to decisions about the sampling. Increasing the sample by adding more weak questions would not make the sampling any better, but adding four good questions would help.

The marks above were invented to illustrate the method. With more pupils, the pattern might be more complex, but if a few questions seem weak, a test may be improved by looking into why they are weak. The idea behind this approach is the basis on which indices of test reliability are calculated. The overall idea is that the more mutually consistent are the test questions, the more confident you can be that simply adding more questions would not make much difference.

References

The list here includes only those studies referred to explicitly in the text.

Black, P., Harrison, C., Hodgen, J., Marshall, M. and Serret, N. (2011) Can teachers' summative assessments produce dependable results and also enhance classroom learning? *Assessment in Education, 18*(4), 451-469

Boyd, B. and Hayward, L. (2008) *Exploring Assessment for Accountability: Report to Scottish Government.* Glasgow: Universities of Strathclyde and Glasgow.

Brookhart, S.M. (2001) Successful students use of formative and summative assessment. *Assessment in Education* 8(2) 153-169.

Connolly, C., Klenowski, V. and Wyatt-Smith, C. M. (2011). Moderation and consistency of teacher judgment: teachers' views. *British Educational Research Journal.* 1, 1-22.

Crisp, V. (2011) The judgement processes involved in the assessment of project work by teachers. Paper read at AEA Europe in Belfast 2011.

Crooks, T. (2011) Assessment for learning in the accountability era: New Zealand. *Studies in Educational Evaluation.* 37(201), 71-77.

Daugherty, R. (2010) Summative assessment by teachers. pp 384-391 in E. Baker, E., B.McGaw and P.Peterson (eds.) *International Encyclopedia of Education* (*3rd Edn.*). London: Elsevier.

Gambell, T. and Hunter, D. (2004) Teacher scoring of large-scale assessment: professional development or debilitation? *Journal of Curriculum Studies*. 36(6), 697-724.

Gunn, S.J. (2007) Literature Review. In C. Wyatt-Smith and G. Masters. *Proposals for a new model of senior assessment: Realising potentials.* Unpublished report prepared for Queensland Studies Authority.

Hallam, S., Kirton, A., Peffers, J., Robertson, P. and Stobart, G. (2004). *Evaluation of project 1 of the assessment is for learning development program: Support for professional practice in formative assessment. Final report.* Available online at: http://www.scotland.gov.uk/library5/education/ep1aldps-00.asp (accessed 1st October 2011).

Harris, L.H. and Brown, G.T.L. (2009) The complexity of teachers' conceptions of assessment: tensions between the needs of schools and students. *Assessment in Education*. 16(3), 363-381.

Hayward, L. et al. (2012) Assessment at Transition: A report produced for the Scottish government. Available on http://www.gla.ac.uk/schools/education/newsandevents/

Hipkins, R. and Robertson, S. (2011). *Moderation and teacher learning: what can research tell us about their inter-relationships?* Wellington, N.Z.: New Zealand Council for Educational Research.

Parr, J.M. and Timperley, H.S. (2008) Teachers, schools and using evidence: Considerations of preparedness. *Assessment in Education*. 15(1), 57-71.

Sadler, D.R. (1987) Specifying and promulgating achievement standards. *Oxford Review of Education*, 13(2), 191-209.

Simon, M. and Forgette-Giroux, R. (2000) Impact of a Content Selection Framework on Portfolio Assessment at the Classroom Level. *Assessment in Education*. 7(1), 83-101.

Webb, D.C. (2009) Designing Professional Development for Assessment. *Educational Designer*. 1(2).

Wyatt-Smith, C. M. and Cumming, J. J. (2003) Curriculum literacies: Expanding domains of assessment. *Assessment in Education*. 10(1), 47-59.

Wyatt-Smith, C.M. and Bridges, S. (2008) *Meeting in the middle – Assessment, pedagogy, learning and students at educational disadvantage.* Evaluation for the Literacy and Numeracy in the Middle Years of Schooling Initiative Strand A. retrieved from http://education.qld.gov.au/literacy/docs/deewr-myp-final-report.pdf

Wyatt-Smith, C., Klenowski, V. and Gunn, S. (2010) The centrality of teachers' judgement practice in assessment: a study of standards in moderation. *Assessment in Education*. 17(1), 59-75.